Food
PUMPKINS

Ernestine Giesecke

Heinemann Library
Chicago, Illinois

Library of Congress Cataloging-in-Publication Data
Giesecke, Ernestine, 1945-
  Pumpkins / Ernestine Giesecke.
      p. cm. -- (Food)
Includes bibliographical references and index.
  ISBN 1-58810-151-7
  1. Pumpkin--Juvenile literature. [1. Pumpkin.] I. Title. II. Series.
  TX401.2.P86 G54 2001
  641.3'562--dc21
                              2001000696

Acknowledgments
Acknowledgements The publisher would like to thank the following for permission to reproduce
photographs: Richard Kolar/Earth Scenes, p.4; Kevin R. Morris/Corbis, p. 5; Andre Jenny/Focus
Group/Picture Quest, p. 6; B. Drake/Photo Link/Photo Disk/Picture Quest, p. 7; Courtesy of The
Pilgrim Society, p. 8; FoodPix, p. 9; Kimberly Saar, p. 10; Dennis Nolan, p. 12; Dwight Kuhn, p. 13;
David Young-Wolff/Photo Edit, p. 14; Dennis Nolan, p. 15; Karen Tweedy Holmes/Corbis, p. 16;
Paul Souders/Corbis, pp. 17, 18; Mary Ann Chastain/AP Photo, p. 19; Courtesy Libbey, pp. 20, 21;
David Young-Wolff/Photo Edit/Photo Quest, p. 22; Phil Borden/Photo Edit, p. 23; USDA, p. 25;
Michael Brosilow/Heinemann Library, p. 26, 27; Agence France Presse/Corbis, p. 28; Myrleen
Ferguson/Photo Edit/Picture Quest, p. 29.

Cover and Title Page Photograph: J. Patton/H. Armstrong Roberts

Some words are shown in bold, **like this.** You
can find out what they mean by looking in the
glossary.

Contents

What Is a Pumpkin?

A pumpkin is a large, round **fruit.** At the top of the pumpkin is a **woody** brown **stem.** People eat the insides of pumpkins.

Some farmers grow pumpkins as a **crop** to sell. Some people grow pumpkins for food and fun.

Kinds of Pumpkins

All pumpkins are orange or yellow on the inside. Most are orange or yellow on the outside, too. But some pumpkins are blue or gray on the outside.

Some pumpkins are very sweet. We use these pumpkins to make pies, puddings, soups, and **side dishes.** Other pumpkins are fed to **livestock,** such as **cattle** and pigs.

In the Past

In North America, Native Americans grew pumpkins along with corn and beans. At the first Thanksgiving in America, the **Iroquois** brought pumpkin to the **settlers.**

The settlers learned how to make **stews,** soups, and desserts with pumpkin. Without these foods, the settlers might not have lived through the winter.

Around the World

People in North and South America have grown pumpkins for thousands of years. Pumpkin may have different names in other countries.

The map shows places in the world that grow the most pumpkins today. Pumpkins grow best in places that have warm summers and chilly winters.

11

Looking at Pumpkins

A pumpkin plant does not grow straight and tall like most other plants. Instead the plant grows on a vine that curls and twists along the ground.

leaves

stem

vine

The outside of a pumpkin is its **rind.** Inside the pumpkin are the **flesh** and seeds. We eat the cooked flesh. Sometimes we even eat the seeds.

seeds   flesh   rind

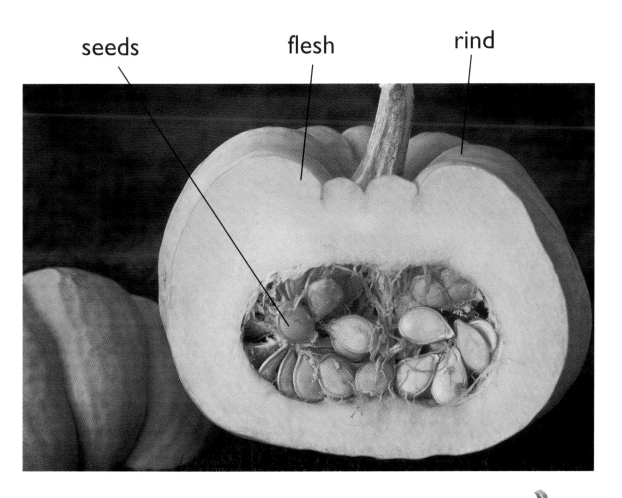

Growing Pumpkins

Each pumpkin grows from a seed. Soon, the seeds begin to grow, or sprout. Next, they produce leaves and then flowers.

Like all plants, pumpkins need sun and **nutrients.** Pumpkins also need lots of space and water.

Bees and Pumpkins

Bees fly to the pumpkin flowers. **Pollen** from the flowers sticks to their bodies. The bees leave some pollen on the next flower they go to. These flowers begin to produce seeds.

Pumpkin **flesh** grows around the seeds. It may take 120 days for a pumpkin to be fully grown. Pumpkins are picked when they are **ripe.**

Canning Pumpkin

On larger farms, the picked pumpkins are shipped to a **cannery.** There, they are **processed** into canned pumpkin.

First, the pumpkins are washed. Next, the pumpkins are **inspected.** Pumpkins that are **bruised** or damaged are thrown away.

19

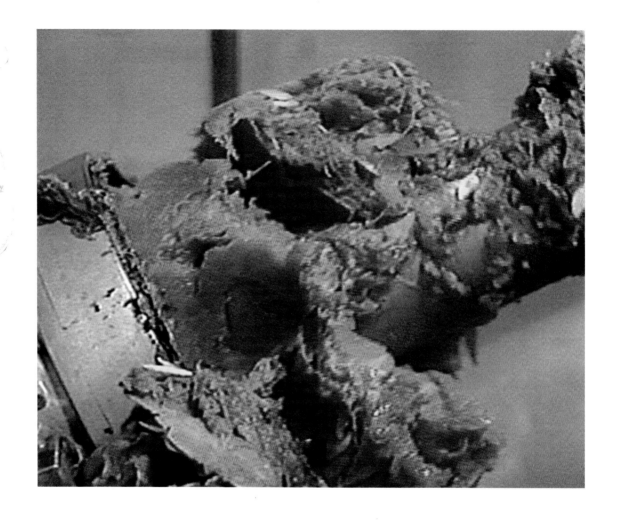

Water is squeezed out of the cooked pumpkin. Then the cooked pumpkin is pushed through a fine **mesh.** This separates the **rind** from the **flesh.**

The cooked pumpkin is then poured into cans. The cans are labeled, packed in cartons, and sent to stores.

Good for You

Pumpkins contain important **nutrients** and **vitamins.** Like other orange-yellow foods, pumpkins have vitamins that can help the body fight off **disease.**

Pies, soups, cakes, and breads are just some of the foods that can be made with pumpkin. Canned pumpkin contains more nutrients than pumpkin that is cooked at home.

Healthy Eating

The food guide **pyramid** shows how much of each different kind of food you should eat every day.

All of the food groups are important, but your body needs more of some foods than others.

You should eat more of the foods at the bottom and the middle of the pyramid. You should eat less of the foods at the top.

Pumpkin is in the **fruit** group. Your body needs two servings of fruit each day.

Fats and Sweets
Eat less

Milk Group
2 servings

Meat Group
2 servings

Vegetable
Group
3 servings

Fruit Group
2 servings

Grain Group   6 servings

Based on the Food Guide Pyramid for Young Children, U.S. Department of
Agriculture, Center for Nutrition Policy and Promotions, March 1999.

25

Pumpkin Recipe

Ask an adult
to help you!

Sweet Pumpkin Dip

2 cups (500 g) powdered sugar
16 ounces (500 g) canned pumpkin
8 ounces (225 g) softened cream cheese
1 teaspoon ground cinnamon
1/2 teaspoon ground ginger
1/4 teaspoon ground cloves
1/4 teaspoon nutmeg

1. Mix all ingredients together in a bowl.

2. Cover the bowl and put it in the refrigerator for an hour.

3. Serve the dip with graham crackers, toast, or fresh fruit.

Pumpkin Fun

In many places there are pumpkin growing contests. People try to grow big pumpkins. This giant pumpkin is nearly as large as the farmer who grew it!

In some cultures, the pumpkin is a **symbol** of **autumn** and the **harvest.** People may carve or decorate pumpkins as part of the celebration.

Glossary

autumn season between summer and winter

bruised mark caused when fruit is roughly handled

cannery place where foods are cooked and put into cans, jars, or bottles

cattle baby and adult cows and bulls

crop plants raised to eat or to sell to others

disease sickness

fat part of some foods that the body uses to make energy and keep warm

flesh part of a fruit that is around the seed, usually the part of the fruit we eat

fruit part of a plant that holds the seeds

grain seed of a cereal plant

harvest gather or bring in fully-grown crops

inspected closely looked at

Iroquois large group of Native American Indian peoples that lived in what is now New York

livestock farm animals such as pigs

mesh open spaces in a screen or net

nutrient food that plants or people need to grow and be healthy

pollen tiny yellow specks on a flower that help make seeds

processed food that is cooked or treated in a certain way to make a new kind of food or drink

pyramid shape with a flat bottom and sides with three edges that come to a point

rind outside skin of some fruits that usually is not eaten

ripe completely grown

settler person who moves to and lives in a new land

side dish food served to go along with the main part of the meal

stem part of a plant that attaches fruit to rest of plant

stew thick mixture of meat, fish, or vegetables

symbol something that stands for an idea

vitamin something the body needs to grow and stay healthy

woody wood-like or tree-like

More Books to Read

Gibbons, Gail. *The Pumpkin Book*. New York: Holiday House, 1999.

Hutchings, Amy. *Picking Apples and Pumpkins*. New York: Scholastic, 1994.

Index